INDEX OF TUNES

		Page
58	A hundred pipers	41
40	A hunting we will go	28
23	•Aiken Drum	21
54	•Blaydon Races	39
39	Bingo	28
1	Bobby Shafto	7
21	•Bricks and mortar	19
4	Buffalo girls	9
30	Click go the shears	25
57	Cock o' the North	41
17	•Coming round the mountain	17
48	Dame get up	33
19	Didn't she ramble	17
51	Feathers	35
42	Fire down below	31
18	Going down town	17
46	Here we go round the mulberry bush	33
53	Here's to the maiden	37
47	Humpty Dumpty	33
34	I can play on the big bass drum	27
2	In and out the windows	7

		Page
36	I've been to Harlem	28
33	I've got a shilling	27
9	Jimmy Allen	11
29	•John Brown's body	25
28	•Ka Foo Zalum	23
26	Keel Row	23
61	Lavender's blue	45
45	Looby Loo	33
7	Little brown jug	9
22	•Lord of the dance	19
43	•Mademoiselle from Armentières	31
11	Muffin man – The	13
59	•My bonny	43
8	My love she's but a lassie	11
25	My mother said	21
63	My rose in June	45
49	Nancy Dawson	35
15	•Nelly Bly	15
60	•Oh dear what can the matter be?	43
14	•Oh Susanna	15
16	•Old Joe Clark	15
6	Old John Braddlum	9

		Page
41	One more river	31
56	Paddy Carey	41
44	Pop goes the weasel	33
50	Quaker's Wife – The	35
20	•Rakes of Mallow	19
12	•Rattling bog – The	13
37	Rise up sugar	28
10	Rose tree – The	11
32	Ten green bottles	27
27	There's nae luck	23
38	There was a jolly miller	28
5	This old man	9
31	•Underneath the spreading chestnut tree	27
35	•Waltzing Matilda	27
62	•Water of Tyne – The	45
13	•What shall we do with the drunken sailor?	13
52	When daylight shines	37
24	When I first came to this land	21
55	When Johnny comes marching home	39
3	•Yankee Doodle Dandy	7

INTRODUCTION

This book of tunes has been compiled to meet the needs of young people who wish to play for English folk dancing. It is suitable for use at folk events, in bands or workshops and also in schools where live music is needed for folk dancing.

The tunes have been selected and arranged so that young people at all levels of musical development can take part without too much teaching and preparation. Those who are already skilled at playing instruments such as recorders, violins and harmonicas, should be able to play the tunes at speed quite easily. Those who have only mastered a few notes or who wish to play percussion instruments can take advantage of the suggestions for second parts or rhythmic accompaniments. It is particularly important that these players should be shown simple ways of participating quickly in the music making. The sooner they can experience the fun of playing in a band, the more likely they are to be inspired to develop their own musical expertise and to undertake the practice that is necessary.

These tunes have been drawn from a number of sources, in particular from other publications of the E F D S S. This means that when the young people begin to use the adult books, they will find familiar tunes that they have played before. The melodies are mostly traditional and many will be recognised easily by dancers and players. The majority can be used equally successfully for adult dances as for those commonly organised for children. A list of suggestions of suitable tunes for different dances is given on page 52. The best introduction to playing for folk dancing is for junior musicians to take part in bands where there are experienced adult players. In some cases, however, children's bands may be formed, but these will usually need strong support from adult musicians in the early stages. This is most usefully given in the form of a violin or accordion lead.

As the tunes are likely to be familiar, a number of players may be able to pick them up by ear. Others will learn them from memory. This is to be encouraged since traditional folk musicians never play for dancing from written music. Playing by ear or from memory enables young people to become more conscious of folk style. In time they may become aware of the limitations of what they are playing and think up ways of elaborating the tune or devising harmonies or second parts. This is an experience of considerable musical value and is quite in keeping with the practice of traditional folk musicians. Once the young players have dispensed with sheet music, they are also in a much better position to watch the dancers. This will enable them to make their music more danceable and also to experience the very special partnership which should exist between players and dancers.

JOIN THE BAND

A selection
of Folk Dance Tunes
for beginners
with second parts

compiled by Barbara Wood

The English Folk Dance and Song Society

CECIL SHARP HOUSE, 2 REGENT'S PARK ROAD, LONDON, NW1 7AY

© COPYRIGHT E F D S S 1974   PRINTED IN ENGLAND

Charity No. 305999   ISBN 0 85418 079 6

REELS

HORNPIPES

BOBBY SHAFTO

IN AND OUT THE WINDOWS

YANKEE DOODLE DANDY

1. BOBBY SHAFTO

2. IN AND OUT THE WINDOWS

3. YANKEE DOODLE DANDY

BUFFALO GIRLS

THIS OLD MAN AND OLD JOHN BRADDLUM

LITTLE BROWN JUG

4. BUFFALO GIRLS

5. THIS OLD MAN

6. OLD JOHN BRADDLUM

These 2 tunes can be played at the same time.

7. LITTLE BROWN JUG

MY LOVE SHE'S BUT A LASSIE

JIMMY ALLEN

THE ROSE TREE

8. MY LOVE SHE'S BUT A LASSIE

9. JIMMY ALLEN

10. THE ROSE TREE

THE MUFFIN MAN

THE RATTLING BOG

WHAT SHALL WE DO WITH THE DRUNKEN SAILOR?

11. THE MUFFIN MAN

12. THE RATTLING BOG

13. WHAT SHALL WE DO WITH THE DRUNKEN SAILOR?

OH SUSANNA

NELLY BLY

OLD JOE CLARK

14. OH SUSANNA

15. NELLY BLY

16. OLD JOE CLARK

COMING ROUND THE MOUNTAIN

Alternative to F♮–G

GOING DOWN TOWN

DIDN'T SHE RAMBLE

17. COMING ROUND THE MOUNTAIN

18. GOING DOWN TOWN

19. DIDN'T SHE RAMBLE

RAKES OF MALLOW

BRICKS AND MORTAR

LORD OF THE DANCE

20. RAKES OF MALLOW

21. BRICKS AND MORTAR

22. LORD OF THE DANCE (Sydney Carter)

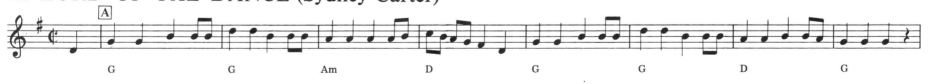

Printed by permission of Galliard Ltd.

AIKEN DRUM

WHEN I FIRST CAME TO THIS LAND

MY MOTHER SAID

23. AIKEN DRUM

24. WHEN I FIRST CAME TO THIS LAND (O. Brand)

Printed by permission of Essex Music Ltd.

25. MY MOTHER SAID

KEEL ROW

May also be used with "Nae Luck"

THERE'S NAE LUCK ABOUT THE HOUSE

May also be used with Keel Row

KA-FOO-ZALUM

26. KEEL ROW

27. THERE'S NAE LUCK ABOUT THE HOUSE

28. KA-FOO-ZALUM

JOHN BROWN'S BODY

CLICK GO THE SHEARS

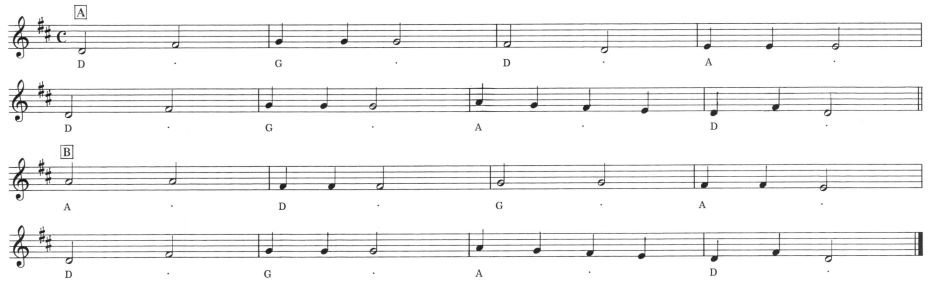

29. JOHN BROWN'S BODY

30. CLICK GO THE SHEARS

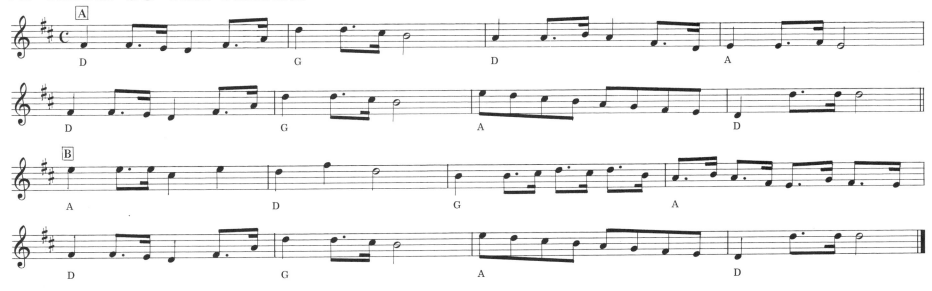

UNDERNEATH THE SPREADING CHESTNUT TREE

TEN GREEN BOTTLES

I'VE GOT A SHILLING

I CAN PLAY ON THE BIG BASS DRUM

WALTZING MATILDA

31. UNDERNEATH THE SPREADING CHESTNUT TREE

32. TEN GREEN BOTTLES

*These tunes can be played together to
make a 16 or 32 bar tune*

33. I'VE GOT A SHILLING

34. I CAN PLAY ON THE BIG BASS DRUM

*These tunes can be played together to
make a 16 or 32 bar tune*

35. WALTZING MATILDA

5 SINGING GAMES

36. I'VE BEEN TO HARLEM

37. RISE UP SUGAR RISE

38. THERE WAS A JOLLY MILLER

39. BINGO

There was a black dog sat on a back porch and Bin-go was his name etc.

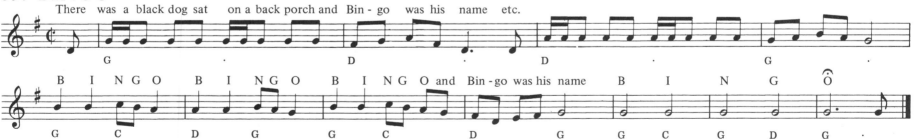

40. A-HUNTING WE WILL GO

JIGS

WALTZES

ONE MORE RIVER

FIRE DOWN BELOW

Alternative to F♮−G

MADEMOISELLE FROM ARMENTIÈRES

41. ONE MORE RIVER

42. FIRE DOWN BELOW

43. MADEMOISELLE FROM ARMENTIÈRES

POP GOES THE WEASEL

LOOBY LOO

HERE WE GO ROUND THE MULBERRY BUSH

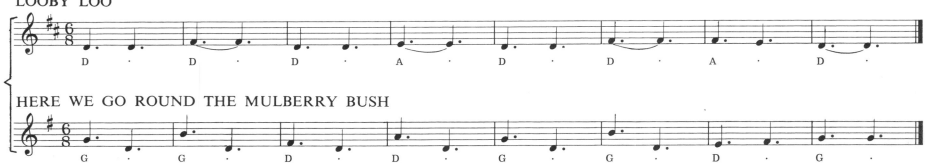

HUMPTY DUMPTY

DAME GET UP AND BAKE YOUR PIES

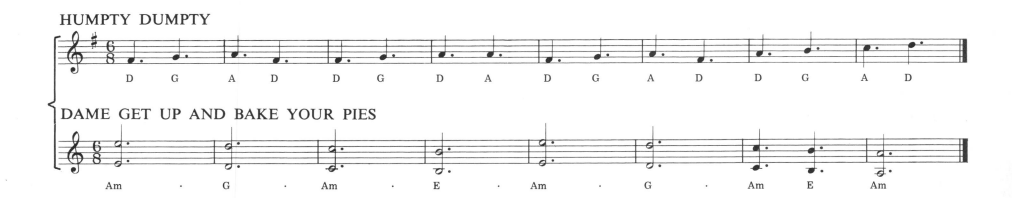

44. POP GOES THE WEASEL

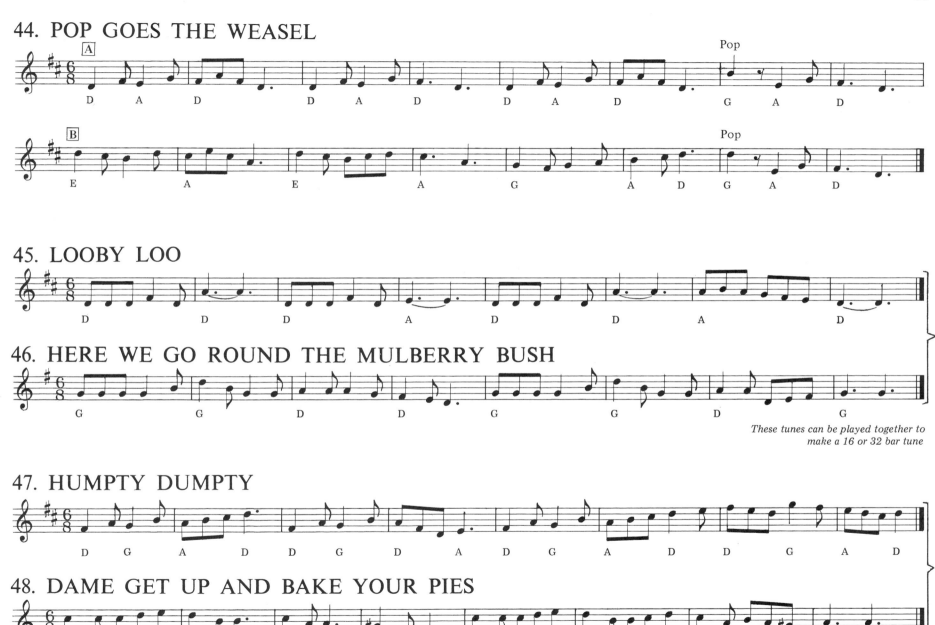

These tunes can be played together to make a 16 or 32 bar tune

45. LOOBY LOO

46. HERE WE GO ROUND THE MULBERRY BUSH

47. HUMPTY DUMPTY

48. DAME GET UP AND BAKE YOUR PIES

These tunes can be played together to make a 16 or 32 bar tune

NANCY DAWSON

THE QUAKER'S WIFE

FEATHERS

49. NANCY DAWSON

50. THE QUAKER'S WIFE

51. FEATHERS

WHEN DAYLIGHT SHINES

HERE'S TO THE MAIDEN

52. WHEN DAYLIGHT SHINES

53. HERE'S TO THE MAIDEN

BLAYDON RACES

WHEN JOHNNY COMES MARCHING HOME

54. BLAYDON RACES

55. WHEN JOHNNY COMES MARCHING HOME

PADDY CAREY

The drones can be played for Cock o' the North and A Hundred Pipers.

COCK O' THE NORTH

A HUNDRED PIPERS

56. PADDY CAREY

57. COCK O' THE NORTH

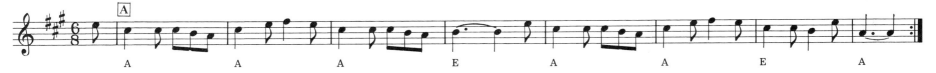

58. A HUNDRED PIPERS

MY BONNY LIES OVER THE OCEAN

OH DEAR, WHAT CAN THE MATTER BE?

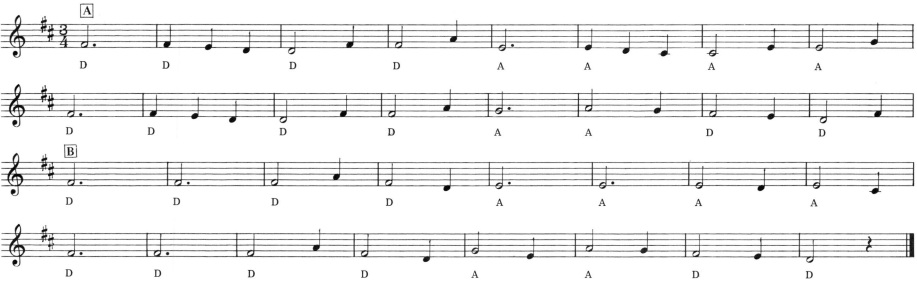

59. MY BONNY LIES OVER THE OCEAN

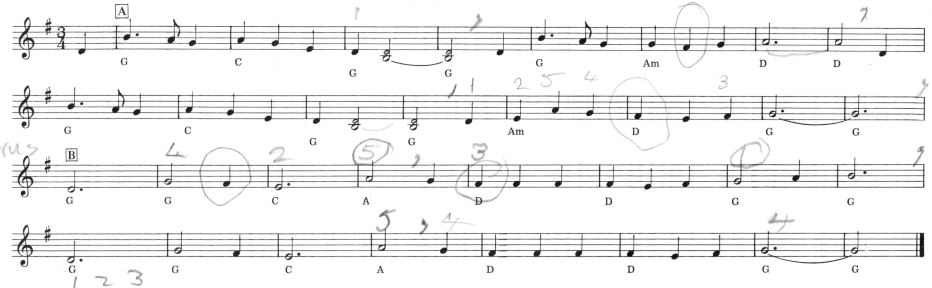

60. OH DEAR, WHAT CAN THE MATTER BE?

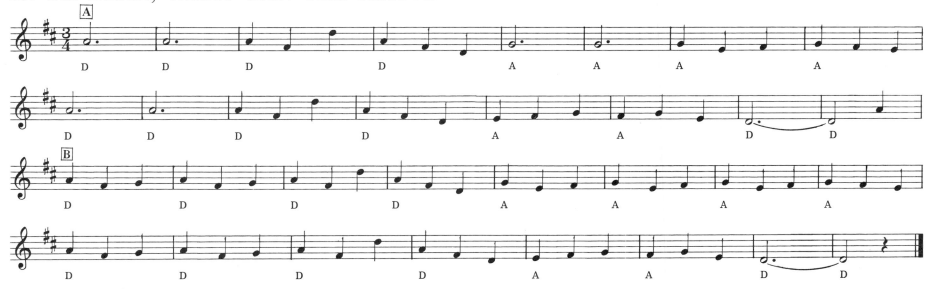

LAVENDER'S BLUE

THE WATER OF TYNE

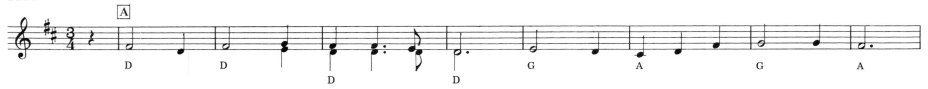

MY ROSE IN JUNE

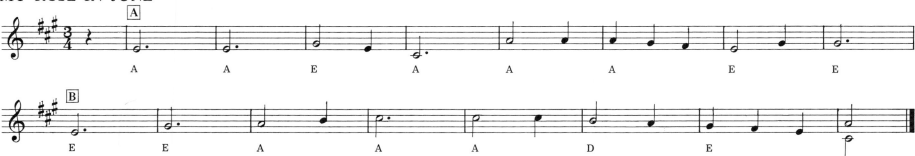

61. LAVENDER'S BLUE

62. THE WATER OF TYNE

63. MY ROSE IN JUNE

Halstan & Co. Ltd., Amersham, Bucks., England

Notes for Leaders

I *The Tune*

The tune is a very important part of English folk dance music and it is vital that it should be heard clearly. It is as well to encourage as many musicians as possible to play the tune since, particularly with young players, it can easily get lost among all the other sounds that are going on. In this book, only the bare bones of the tunes have been given to simplify sight reading. Attempts to improvise, add passing notes and otherwise decorate, should be encouraged as long as the character of the melody is not destroyed. It is useless to try to describe the style in which tunes should be played. Young people should have as many opportunities as possible of hearing good traditional musicians, preferably live, but if not, on record or tape.

The tunes are mostly written in the keys of G D and A. Young violin players are usually more at home in the keys of D and A, while players of most other instruments used for folk music find the key of G easier. The second parts are so arranged, that where the key presents difficulty, young players will be able to join in with notes that are familiar. Sometimes the speed of the tune is too fast for beginners and they may find that the tempo of the second part is more easily manageable.

Good melody instruments are:-
  violins, harmonicas, melodicas, concertinas, recorders, melodeons, pipes, accordions (right hand), flutes.

N.B. Although the piano can be used to supplement the tune when the situation is desperate, it is generally better to regard it as a percussive instrument in folk dance music. It can often give a very steady foundation to the musical sound of the band by providing an effective bass line in the left hand (cf. double bass) and a variety of rhythmic percussive effects in the right (see notes on 'the bass line'.)

II *The Second Parts*

The second parts have been arranged with simplicity, rather than musical interest in mind. They are meant to be unobtrusive and complementary to the tune and should never be allowed to dominate it. Many of them are in the form of an ostinato or have a repetitive rhythm. Instruments such as recorders, accordions and concertinas can often be very penetrating and should play these parts with restraint. Where large numbers of young people wish to play the second parts on these instruments, it should be arranged for them to alternate each time through the tune. In some cases, the parts are written so that the violins can play lower notes than are possible on recorders. This is usually suggested where the tune is easy for recorders to play and more difficult for violins. Quite young children can often play the second parts on xylophone or glockenspiels. They will generally not be able to read the music at the same time but will learn the parts by remembering the visual pattern of the notes. It is sometimes helpful for the adult to demonstrate the parts to these children. Word patterns have been suggested for some of the second parts. The adult or the children themselves can make up their own word patterns for the others. If the children repeat these patterns to themselves, they can usually keep the rhythm going without too much difficulty. The second parts are not, of course, exhaustive. Adults can alter and adapt them to suit the needs of the young people in the band. It might sometimes be necessary to make them even simpler. In this case, the young people could just play the note as indicated by the letters under each bar. There is also no reason why young people should not elaborate or devise their own second parts, providing they listen very carefully to see whether they "suit" the tune.

III *The Harmonies*

These can be played on guitars, accordion and melodeon basses, piano and sometimes on glockenspiels. So as not to confound the young players, only the basic I IV V harmonies and occasional relative minors have been suggested. This has meant that some rules of harmony have been broken, but the chords will sound perfectly acceptable in context. It is an exceptional child under ten or eleven years who can distinguish between quite simple harmonies, and it is therefore better to concentrate on basic differences at this stage. This does not, of course, prevent adults from playing more sophisticated harmony themselves and from teaching further refinements to gifted young people who are interested. If the players find difficulty in reading the changes in harmony, they may be helped by colouring in bars according to the way in which they are harmonised;

IV *The Bass Line*

This can be a very important feature of the musical sound of the band since it is often the one that can be heard most clearly when there is a crowd of boisterous dancers. It is normally played on a double bass, but the same kind of effect can be made with a 'cello, electric guitar or piano. A very simple bass line can be devised by playing the tonic note of the chords suggested for the harmony (i.e. the letters that are written below the notes). Where there are dots (under the second parts), these notes can be repeated or other notes in that chord can be substituted.

e.g. G · / G · / D · /   can be played

G B / G D / D A /
(3rd)   (5th)   (5th)

This line can be made even more interesting and tuneful by changing the tonic notes which are written, for others in the chord and by adding passing notes and other runs. Only a few young people will manage this and most would probably be helped if the whole line were written out in full by the adult. It is important to remember that the piano is not the prerogative of adults and that young pianists can be very successful at playing a simple bass note–chord accompaniment.

V Rhythm

A rhythmic accompaniment can add an exciting dimension to dance music. It is important that it should be sympathetic to the phrasing of the melodies. This frequently presents problems with junior musicians. Young children in particular like to join the rhythm section, and junior bands are often overweighted with "tappers" and "shakers", most of whom have little musical experience. These young players, however, should not be discouraged and the following suggestions for organising them might be helpful.

1. Only allow suitable instruments

Standard percussion instruments (e.g. drums and tambourines) are acceptable as long as not more than one or two of each are used. Avoid cymbals, tin drums and gongs!

Home made instruments often have much quieter sounds and more can be included. The following are useful; shakers and maraccas of all kinds, claves (two wooden sticks), small jingle sticks (broom handles with bottle tops loosely nailed on), bamboo sticks with notches and a scraper, bells (morris bells would do), anything that will tap, rattle or scrape. Encourage the young people to experiment and to think of their own ideas.

2. Group the instruments by sound

There is no one way of doing this, but it is helpful to put the "tappers", the "shakers", the "ringers" and the "scrapers" in separate groups. Remember that the harmonic rhythmic instruments such as accordion, basses, guitars and glockenspiels form a separate group. Then the different groups can take turns in playing tunes and phrases.

This keeps the noise level moderate and adds variety to the sound.

3. Before beginning to play, encourage the young people to explore the possibilities of their instrument

Many young people do not realise that;

a. Instruments can be played *softly* as well as loudly.

b. One instrument can make several different sounds (i.e. it can be scraped, tapped and rattled). Sometimes different parts of the instrument make different sounds.

It is worth playing some preliminary tunes while the players experiment with their instruments. Younger children enjoy the game situation, where the leader calls whether the tune is to be played loudly, softly, with taps, shakes etc. Some children like to set up a "one man band" with a number of different percussive sounds. This often appeals to older children and teenagers with limited musical interest or experience.

4. Make sure the young people are aware of different rhythmic patterns

The tunes in this book have been divided into 2 sections according to rhythm;

(a) reels and hornpipes

(b) jigs and waltzes

Some young people find it difficult to distinguish between reels and jigs and it might be helpful if they are referred to as;

(a) walking (or running) rhythms   (reels)

(b) skipping rhythms   (jigs)

The leader should get the young people playing a very simple rhythm e.g. ♩ ♪♩ ♪ for jigs. When this is established, the tune can be played over the top. Gradually the young people will become more adventurous and think of variations. The rhythmic word patterns which are written over some of the second parts and which can be devised for others, may help to suggest ways in which the rhythm can be varied. It is worth encouraging the players to think of ways of adding interest to the end of a tune or as one phrase or melody leads into another.

Again, it is impossible to indicate all that should be said about good rhythmic playing. There is no substitute for listening critically and carefully to good bands with sensitive, supporting rhythm sections. The fundamental principle is that players in this section should enhance the rhythmic, danceable quality of the tune, taking great care not to dominate, to flatten or to overtake the melody.

Suggested Tunes for dances

For many dances jigs and reels are interchangeable. Try using tunes other than those suggested. Be careful, however, to check the length of the dance carefully and work out the number of phrases needed. Most tunes have two 8 bar phrases. The first is usually called the A music, the second the B music. Sometimes there is a third phrase of 8 bars called the C music. In this book several 8 bar tunes are included. They are usually coupled with another 8 bar tune and the two tunes can be played together as a 16 or 32 bar tune. Where tunes are written without a repeat at the end of the A music, it is probably better to play A B A B instead of A A B B for 32 bar tunes.

		Pages
American longways or square dances	A B or A A B B	15, 17
A hunting we will go	original	28
Belfast Duck	A B	25
	8 bar tunes twice each	27
Bingo	original	28
Blaydon Races	original (and When Johnny comes)	39
Bonnets so blue	A B B	35
Brighton Camp	A B B	11
Butterfly	A B B	13
Circassian circle	A A B B	19, 31
Circle Waltz	A B	43
	A B A B	45
Cumberland reel	A A B B	31, 33, 35
Cumberland square eight	A A B B	11
Durham Reel	A B (5 times)	41
Haste to the wedding (Hereford)	A A A B B	41
Here we go round the mulberry bush	original	33
Hullichan roundabout	A B	31, 33, 35, 37
I can play on the big bass drum	original	27
I've been to Harlem	original	28
La Russe	A A B B	7, 13
	4 tunes each played twice (or return to original for 4th tune)	

		Pages
Long eight	A A B B	31, 33, 35, 37
Long sword dancing	A A B B	7
Looby Loo	original	33
Lucky seven	A A B B	31, 33, 35, 37
Muffin man	original	13
Mulberry bush	original	33
Ninepins	A A B	41
	stop suddenly when all the men or women are in the middle	
Nottingham Swing	A A B B	23
	A B	25, 27
Pat-a-cake Polka	A B	9
Rant dances (e.g. Dorset Ring)	A A B B or as directed	19, 21
Rise up sugar rise	original	28
Sicilian circle	A A B B	7, 13, 15, 17 31, 33, 35, 39
The rose tree	A A B B	11
There was a jolly miller	original	28
Three meet	A A B B	37
Triple promenade	A A B B	13, 15, 17 31, 33, 35, 39
Trip to the cottage	A A B B or A A B C	31, 33, 35, 37
Virginia reel	A A B B twice (longer version) or A A B B B simple version	7, 13, 15, 17 31, 33, 35
Waltz country dance	A B repeat last 8 bars	43
	A B A B B	45